Change Soup
Leading Inspired Change

Jeff Flesher, PhD

For Bonnie, rolling with the changes

Table of Contents

Change Your Life?

Will this book change your life? It just might. Maybe you are reading this book because you are responsible for making the soup of change, or maybe you feel like you're up to your chin in the most recent batch of change soup cooked up where you work and live. Either way, I believe that this story can change your life, and that is why I share it with you. My goal is to tell a simple story that can help make sense of what is happening and make it easier to be effective as you lead change.

There are many stories about management and change. There is at least some truth in all of them. The truth in this story is the result of my personal leadership practice and need to understand and influence change. It is based on my efforts to make practical sense of what we know, and apply that in leading my teams and guiding others.

In a very real sense this is my personal Change Soup cookbook. My recipe learned through years of study and application. My hope is that as you read the book you will make connections and take with you those new ingredients that make sense for the next version of your personal recipe for success.

One of the core problems with change management is that we treat it as a special problem to be solved. We pull out a system of processes and communication templates when we are working on a really big project. We assign these duties to someone while others do the real work of pushing the project through to completion. We meet with limited success because the change efforts are not aligned with the project, are too complex, and often start too late to make any real difference.

Change is an ongoing natural condition for all of us. It is the single most important thing we do in our organizations. Leaders at all levels are expected on a regular basis to make change happen. We are asked to make more value, create more profit, and find the new and innovative methods and products that will lead to a more successful future.

Our environment is a constant flux and flow of new people, new systems, and process revisions. We also navigate all the good ideas that are supposed to help us improve and prepare for the future. Some of these ideas are our own and others might be imposed on us from senior leaders, boards, or external forces. In any case we are there to make sense of it and make it happen.

Creating and navigating change is the fundamental work of leadership

We usually don't have the luxury of an obvious reason to change that everyone will just naturally support. We know that sometimes the outcomes will be negative for us and others. There are also times where there is no choice. As leaders we must be able to get in front of pending changes so that we can show others the way. We are expected to be role models so that others can follow us.

Everyone can lead change. We all have to do it, even if only on a personal level. To be a leader doesn't require managerial titles, senior positions, or even direct reports. As members of an organization we are all responsible for realizing goals, escalating issues and modifying plans to fit reality. Our understanding of change and our personal change resilience will determine the outcomes we achieve.

This is serious and important work. People depend on us to see the way forward, to have good judgement and limit the inherent risk of our choices. No one can predict the future but the good news is that there are some simple things we can do to increase our odds for personal and organizational success. We can leverage proven methods to be better prepared and more resilient. That is the purpose of this book.

Chapter One
What do we know about Change?

Is it positive? Negative? Both? For most people the answer is it depends, which it turns out is the answer to lots of important questions. There are changes in life that most of us would agree are negative like the loss of a loved one, financial trouble or losing our jobs. These events represent turning points in our lives and significant adjustments to our relationships, hopes and dreams. But it's not just the negative changes in life that are difficult. Even very positive changes can cause major stress and worry.

If you have children, think back to the time close to your first child's birth. You likely were filled with anticipation, looking forward to this wonderful event. The beautiful baby to love, cuddle and nurture, to share your life and make your family complete. You probably also had feelings of concern. How would you care for them? What would you do if there were problems? How would you afford all of those diapers?

Another example would be starting a new job. You have the excitement for a new opportunity and the joy at the new salary, or location. But at the same time you worry about being able to perform to unknown expectations, having to learn all of the new systems and figuring out a new boss.

Change is growth, and achievement and accomplishment. It is fun and challenging and exciting. It is also death, separation, crisis and ruin. It is disillusionment and fearful and bad. That's right; it's all of those things and more. If you hang around long enough chances are you'll get to see many of these faces of change.

Just as the changes we experience are diverse, the way we experience change is also multifaceted. Some people love change and actively seek it out. They pay money to go to scary movies, or on exotic trips, or engage in extreme sports for the thrill of it all. Others prefer a sedate life. Vacation is a staycation in the garden or going to the same favorite spot every year. Some like to try new restaurants, others stick with the tried and true. Some of us just seem wired for change while others seem to be naturally more fearful or hesitant.

If I asked you to tell me about your life experience you might tell me about where you have lived, jobs and school, accomplishments and maybe even some setbacks. When we tell each other about ourselves we typically talk in terms of change, "I went to college here, I worked there, and we had these children." In fact from birth we have adapted and sought change. It is as natural as anything. As a species we are really quite good at it evidenced by the billions of us living in almost every part and condition on earth.

The story of our lives is the story of our changes

A personal example

Most children are fearless. They explore and learn because it is fun. We are naturally curious and our lives depend on growing (changing) to adapt to our environments. Somewhere along the way we start to learn to be more cautious. We hear "don't touch that it will burn you" probably yelled by our frantic parents. We have experiences that don't go well and we imprint that memory. We tell ourselves "Don't do that again."

We have all seen people react to change with excitement, fear, acceptance and resistance. When I think back about the changes I've experienced I'm sure I've had all of these reactions and more. Change typically initiates a primordial fear response. Our automatic protection is fight or flight. It is automatic. It brings the energy of strong emotion and adrenalin. Good things to have when faced with a hungry lion, less great in a big meeting with everyone watching and judging our performance.

In the workshops I teach on change, I like to share a personal experience. It is my representative example of a major change. I was part of a group of about thirty who had just joined a new organization. I didn't want to be there. I was afraid. I didn't know anyone, and the reactions from the people in the group were all over the place. It was crazy.

My kindergarten class

Yes, that's me in the circle. I appear to be staring at the cute little girl in front of me, of course this was before I was married.

Kindergarten was my first real experience away from home. It was mandated by the state of Indiana for my own good and the greater good of society at large. I did not request to go, or as I remember see any need. I was perfectly happy at home with my mom, our dog, and playing with the neighborhood kids. Suddenly I was dealing with new rules, people I didn't know, and scary stories of a large paddle in the principal's office that might be used at any time.

Of course a funny thing happened during that year. With no formal change management that I'm aware of, I adapted. My class mates became my friends, my first crush, and my window into other families. Like most little kids, I loved my teacher. I never saw the paddle and the Principal was a fine person and neighborhood leader. To my knowledge we all succeeded that year, and most of us went on to finish our compulsory education with fond memories and many valuable lessons learned.

One of my favorite activities back then was Storytime. We would all gather around to listen to the teacher read one of our favorite books. I think that was right before nap time. I still like to read and take a nap; she was a really good teacher! Many of the books that she would read were classic fairy tales or fables. These stories had heroes and princesses and almost always a moral or two.

I think most people are drawn to stories, we love to watch TV and go to the movies and even our music tends to be the three minute versions of conflict, redemption, good times and bad. Or to put it another way – they are stories about change. The morals are advice for when we find ourselves in similar situations. Sometimes the meaning is shaded or has multiple levels to discover. Let me share one of my favorites from back then with you now.

Chapter Two

The fable of Stone Soup, a story about Inspired Change

One of the stories I remember from kindergarten is Stone Soup. Like most fables there are several versions and the origin is obscure although the basic plot is the same. Stone Soup is a story about three hungry soldiers and the magic way they made and shared a feast with a small village.

It was a time of war and hardship. The three soldiers were returning home and on the way passed through a small village. The soldiers were hungry. They didn't have anything to eat so they asked at several homes only to be turned away by all of the villagers. Times were difficult for everyone and there was hardly enough in any household to take care of themselves let alone three strangers.

Eventually the soldiers gave up but they didn't move on. Instead they went to the village green and placed their cooking pot filled with water on a fire to boil. As you might suspect, in a small village the word got around and people were suspicious of what the soldiers were up to so a few started to gather around to ask them what they were doing.

The soldiers told them that they had asked for food at all of the houses but no one had anything to spare. Because the village was in such dire need, the soldiers had decided to use one of their last magic stones to create a feast. The soldiers were going to prepare this meal and share it with the entire village.

Excitement went through the village and soon everyone had crowded around to see this magic and share in the feast. As the water started to boil, one of the soldiers pulled from his bag a smooth stone. "This is a magic stone which we can use to create the most wonderful meal, Stone Soup." "We have made this for the King and it is his favorite meal of all." With that he gently let the stone slip into the caldron and said, "Now just watch."

In a moment one of the other soldiers said, "I remember one time when we had stone soup and it was particularly good because we added a few potatoes." Hearing this one of the villagers volunteered that he did have some potatoes and ran to get them to add to the soup.

Now, the first soldier acknowledged that potatoes were good in the soup, but he remembered once when carrots and onions had been added. That was his favorite version. Two villagers stepped forward. One said she would get some carrots and the other said he had a few good onions to add. Both hurried off to get their ingredients.

"Well," said the third soldier. "I have had many stone soups and I think the best I ever ate had a bit of beef." In a moment another villager offered that yes, they had some beef they could add. Now this continued through several more ingredients and almost everyone had something they could add to the soup or bring to accompany the dish.

In the end, they really did have a meal fit for a king and everyone shared in the feast. After eating the soldiers thanked the villagers for their contributions and the first soldier said, "We have two more magic stones and each can be used many times, therefore since you have been so generous we will leave you this stone." He said, "You can make this feast whenever you like and I must say that this version today was truly the best any of us ever had."

The villagers were very happy and a vowed to make stone soup again soon. The soldiers bade them farewell and went about their journey home with full stomachs and a twinkle in their eyes.

The morale of the story back in kindergarten was about sharing and working together. A pretty good point to make with five year-olds who were inclined to fight over every treasured toy, best friend playmate, and the teacher's attention. Later, though I realized that this story has a deeper meaning, it is about leading inspired change.

So what does this story have to do with change? The basic change the soldiers wanted was from nothing to eat to full stomachs. The three soldiers wanted something very dear from a village made up of people they didn't know who thought they had nothing to give. But in the end they achieved their goal by engaging the entire village in a magical event that left everyone satisfied and happy. Not only that, they also left them the hopeful promise of continued success. Not a bad day's work.

Thinking about the story, let's answer a few questions.

Who were the leaders? The soldiers are the leaders in this story. They have a personal goal to get something to eat. They lead the entire village to accomplish their intention.

What did they bring? They brought the goal with a clear understanding of what they wanted and the commitment to not give up too quickly. They also had multiple approaches to get it done.

What did the people bring? Everything needed to achieve the goal itself, all of the ingredients.

How did they inspire change? Through an engaging story, believing in themselves and extending that belief to the people of the village.

I'm sure you can see some of the change connections and maybe even more than I've outlined. Doesn't it sound familiar? We lead groups, formally or informally where we are trying to accomplish something. Maybe we're not sure it can be done. There are good reasons for failure and maybe the first try doesn't work. But our job is to find a way to get others to make their contributions and accomplish our desired changes.

Now you might say the soldiers tricked the villagers into doing what they wanted, and that would be a fair point. The soldiers also saw more potential and opportunity than the village could see themselves at that moment. Sound familiar? They started by believing that it could be done and in the process they shared a confidence that the group made its own.

I find the inspiration part of the story to be my favorite part. The soldiers choose an inspirational path – the magic stone story. They had other choices. It wasn't their first choice. Remember they went to all of the houses and just asked. If anyone had given them something to eat it would have been the end of the story but that didn't work so they needed to regroup. They could have ordered the people to give them food. Maybe they could have even forced them to do it. Those things would have worked, they would have accomplished the goal, but not in a way that the soldiers wanted to share.

In the end their choice of an inspirational approach not only accomplished the goal but through encouraging all of the villager's contributions, it exceeded their desires. It was not a complex plan but it did have an effective framework. There wasn't a burning platform for motivation but there was a compelling story. The people became excited to contribute what they had. The goal was accomplished and everyone shared in the reward. When the feast was over the soldiers also left a legacy; a new method and the confidence for the people to share in the future.

Below are a few change related morals to the story. In the following sections of this book we will explore them in more depth. We will elaborate on these as our own magic recipe to make Change Soup whenever we want.

A Moral or two from the story

Understand the situation and people

Have a clear **intention** – know what done looks like

Inspire engagement and involvement

Have an **approach**, plan, or method but be flexible

Sustain – leave confidence and competence

Believe – In yourself, in your goal, and in your group

Chapter Three
Understand

Attributions and Assumptions

I'm sure you have had the experience where you thought you saw a person you know, only to get closer and find that you were wrong. One of the primary ways we think is through matching patterns. It is efficient and enables us to be able to recognize and react quickly. When we think we see a pattern we jump to the conclusion that goes with it.

Understanding the assumed framework (patterns) around our situation is the first step in cooking Change Soup. There are two types of patterns that are especially influential. What we think happened and why – our attributions, and what we expect will happen and the boundaries for our actions – our assumptions. This applies to us and all the other actors in our situation.

We are discovering attributions when we hear someone say, "Let me tell you the history of this." To make sense of the world we create attributions, or reasons, for why things happened even when we don't have a clue. It is natural, it happens all the time and it can be very inaccurate. If our attributions are wrong we misdiagnose root causes and end up creating solutions for the wrong problems.

Here's an example I've seen in most of my leadership jobs. Early in my new role my direct reports tell me about the employees I should fire. I generally respond in the same way, "If you knew they should be fired why didn't you do it before I got here?" I've never gotten a good answer to that question. What tends to be true is that someone made a mistake and people started to doubt them. It became a vicious cycle of mistrust and lowered expectations. In almost all of these situations my new perspective and normal expectations was all that was needed for them to get back on track.

Sometimes our assumptions and observations give us opposite information. We have one change assumption that tells us that people are afraid, unwilling and will resist change. At the same time we maintain that we are highly adaptable, know how to do this naturally, and actually enjoy change. Both are true. This is why a simple problem solving approach to change is often not successful. Change is not a problem to solve; it is a constant state to prepare for, influence and navigate.

A choice you have to make is what core assumptions and attributions will you choose and practice to help you personally with change and to guide others. I'll suggest a few that I have found helpful, they are rooted in my own study and practice. Use what works for you and add your own tried and true starters for your change soup.

I like to start with a few framing biases (assumptions). I know that they are not always true but they tend to be generally directionally correct. These are my useful biases. Think of these as the water in my Change Soup pot. In fact, being directionally correct, in the ballpark, is my framing bias for overall goals. Many efforts get off-track due to false precision in the expected outcomes. We may be able to calculate an expected ROI but we should never expect it to be extremely accurate from the start. Usually we don't exactly know how it will work; we must reserve some flexibility and start.

A second related assumption is that while we need to understand our objective and possible end state, the most important goal is often the next step, not the last step. We need to get going and to gain momentum. To learn as we go, to pull more people in and be open to tweaking based on the collective wisdom and our experience. Great leaders can see stepping stones along the path.

We also need an operational assumption about human behavior and motivation. I've found it to be very useful to assume that most people come to work with a desire to be successful. Most people want to do the right thing. We know some don't but we can't allow the few bad instances to control how we treat everyone. What kind of leader would you want? A suspicious person who sows doubt or one who starts by giving you the benefit of the doubt?

A general assumption that I'm sharing with you in this book is choosing to be inspirational. More about that later as I believe it is central to our success. Our behavior, relationships, and treatment of others are our strongest tools in creating change success. These are to a great extent under our control. I believe more change recipes fail from poor cooks than bad ingredients.

The last framing assumption for now is related to the extension of the general good intent most people try to bring to their work and lives. I like to think of this as the good idea bias. There is a conflict of good ideas and it is everywhere. There are a million ways to do things. We generally can't prove they will work or not until we try. I like to assume that all ideas are good but they may not be the best match right now for this situation. So in general it's not an argument about the value of any idea. I'll admit they are all potentially useful. What we need to do now is to decide what good idea is the best solution for the situation at hand.

Change is not a problem to solve; it is a constant state to prepare for, influence and navigate

Change Readiness

We can think of change readiness as the potential for effective change within a person and group. That doesn't mean it will be easy or that there won't be disagreements. Some of the influences for change readiness are very difficult to control or modify but we can bias ourselves toward success through influencing actions.

Think of readiness like a garden plot or field. If we turn the soil, add fertilizer, water and remove the weeds we are much more likely to have the harvest we expect. Of course along the way we will need to manage our garden to some degree to help keep things on track but it is very likely that the initial preparation will define the end results.

The basis for group readiness is the readiness of the individual team members and our own selves. Some of us have had generally positive experiences with change and if that is the case we likely will have a belief that change is OK. If on the other hand our experience has been negative, we are more likely to have a negative reaction. There are other factors that contribute to how we feel about change beyond our perceived loss or benefit. These include the nature of the change itself, our degree of involvement, our temperament and personal attitudes, and our core beliefs about life.

We have already mentioned that some people just seem to be wired for change. They actively seek it and while that can be helpful it can also lead to impatience and a penchant for chasing shiny objects. Others have a temperament that is more cautious. They want to be sure before proceeding and can get stuck in the details and myriad of what-ifs that cloud any situation.

I find it useful to recognize that these somewhat opposite temperaments and everything in between contribute to the differences that make us individuals. I also assume that it is very hard to change. I can't send people to a training class or ask them to read a book and expect that their ingrained personality and core beliefs will change overnight. This doesn't mean we ignore the effects of temperament. It is important that team members be able to adhere to general group norms and develop a willingness to try.

This leads to another important assumption we need to make about our role in leading change. We are not there to make everyone happy. Sometimes we won't be happy either. This is one of the most difficult aspects of leading change. We are good people; we want the best for our teams and ourselves but we need to realize the limitations of our roles and power. Like it or not, life is ups and downs. So is work.

I can hear people saying as they read this last paragraph, "What? I always strive to be fair and I take care of my people." I'm not suggesting that the way forward is to be an insensitive jerk. Soon our discussion will turn toward being inspirational change leaders but for now let's be grounded. We shouldn't try to fool ourselves and we won't be able to fool others.

We have the power to be respectful, understanding, consistent with our values, even-tempered and inspirational, but we can't make people happy or live their lives. We need to be aware of how people react and do our best to support and help them. We also need to remember that we are in roles primarily to accomplish organizational goals and to move forward in the agreed direction. We need to understand that direction, have our concerns and questions answered so we can help others, and lead the way.

Our core outlook on life also contributes to our change bias. We all know people who we would call "glass half full" people. When they are involved in a change they naturally look for the advantages and have a confidence that, "this will all work out and I'll be OK." On the other hand, the glass half empty person might look at changes as threats. This is another opportunity for disaster and they see all of the possible ways that this will hurt them.

I've even had discussions with groups about change where I think some of the people didn't even have a glass! These are the folks who have become so jaded, disillusioned and distrustful that all they can see is negativity and often they want to share that with everyone else.

Whatever it is, it's catching

Certainly one thing that is true in groups, whether families or at work, is that emotions are contagious. When we are around people who are down and negative it rubs off. It is uncomfortable. But the opposite is also true, if we are part of a group that is positive, or with a positive person, that is catching too. What happens if you are walking down the street and someone smiles at you? I bet that in most cases you smile back, this natural response is an example of this effect.

Here is where we get to the counterbalance of our earlier statements about fairness and making people happy. We can't make them happy but we do need to take the responsibility for role modelling the behavior we expect and intervening when the energy is trending too negatively. One of the most powerful readiness components is group think and peer pressure. We should not ignore it or leave the outcomes to chance.

At this point we must acknowledge another aspect of individual change readiness. Sometimes it doesn't work. This can be due to individual choice, change weariness, or fundamental disagreement with our direction. It can also be because the future needs of the organization don't match previous roles and contributions. This can lead to a displacement or reassignment. There is no question to me that this is the hardest part of leadership.

In one company I worked in we used to talk about the people who were practicing to quit. It was like they were waiting for the right time or for another job to come through. I have made it my practice not to hold this against anyone as long as they can maintain performance and manage the negativity. I understand that I need to respect that sometimes people are making difficult choices and sometimes they work through it and stay.

As much as I would like this story to only have good endings, sometimes it doesn't. Accepting the challenge of leadership means accepting the need to be the bringer of good and bad news and responsible for both types of action. It is critical that we learn to make peace with our work. I remember the first time I was part of letting go a group of employees. The stress led to chest pains that took me to the cardiologist. Luckily it was just stress and I learned that in this situation the best I could do was to be respectful, consistent and follow the rules.

Sometimes we find ourselves in situations where our options are very limited. As a young man I served on a submarine. Submarines have a well-earned reputation for having great food. One of our cooks was a wonderful baker and I always looked forward to the homemade cinnamon rolls he made. Not only was he a great baker but also inadvertently a great teacher who taught me something about change.

In those days there was no mail or outbound communication, just a few telegram like messages called family grams. Family members were cautioned to be careful in what they said to avoid upsetting the crew and told that messages would be censored if they included bad news given that it might be weeks before we could reply. Somehow, our baker got a message from his wife that she was leaving him. He was devastated. Soon I noticed an effect on my cinnamon rolls. I became upset and decided I had to say something to him. His response to me was, "Go eat somewhere else."

Years later with some better understanding I know that if I were in this situation again I would be a better friend and do what I could to help. Maybe I could have even learned to make the rolls. I do appreciate the life lesson he taught me. Sometimes we have no choice in the situation, but we always have a choice in how we treat and support each other as we experience life's ups and downs.

We always have a choice

Building Readiness

In a very basic sense we can think of management activity as a basic cycle of doing things and getting ready to do more or different things. We have today's work and the need to be ready for tomorrow. The good news is that in all of our current work there are embedded opportunities to create readiness for the future.

Change readiness is created by what we do every day. The routine management and maintenance of performance - people, processes, and systems will enable change or impeded it. Let's look at some areas that are key drivers of performance and change readiness. We can think of these as some of the key ingredients for our Change Soup. We will need to maintain freshness and good quality to be ready to make our next batch.

Priority

Priority is more than just goals and strategy. It is maintaining a real-time alignment with what is important. Sifting the wheat of useful activities from the chaff of wasted effort and distraction. It is expressed through expectations and confirmed by the understanding the team has of direction. A key to success is doing important work, priority setting keeps us on track.

Clarity

When we talk about change we often emphasize the importance of communication. We talk about the need for repetition in messages, alignment, and confirmation that messages were received. I like to look at this a little differently. Communication is the method, clarity is the desired result. Clarity is the accurate understanding of what is going on, who can help, what we are supposed to do, and what to do when it doesn't work.

Think back to when you started at a new job. You had to learn a new language of organizationally specific definitions for terms and acronyms. You also had to make sure you quickly understood the cultural norms and behavioral expectations to avoid early missteps. On top of that you had to figure out how to do the job.

Clarity is understanding the organizational expectations from every direction and source. We have norms and goals, SOP's and work instructions, verbal direction, emails, and project charters to name a few. We are responsible to filter, elaborate and reinforce these messages for our teams. Remember to make things as simple and easy as possible. Even the most complex things can be broken down, main points lead to more detail, questions and answers lead to understanding.

Feedback

Much of what we do in organizational systems and management is based on a simple loop between expectations and feedback. We tell someone what we want, we later check to see if it happened. We develop goals and then have periodic reviews. The challenge with feedback is often taking the time to make sure it is effective.

There are two types of feedback; corrective and diagnostic. Diagnostic feedback tells us if we are right or wrong. Corrective feedback gets us back on track when we have made errors. Diagnostic feedback is easier. It is much less difficult to see that a result does not hit the target than to take the time to coach someone to performance.

Feedback is what makes learning and practice work. If we practice without feedback we may just reinforce poor methods and outcomes. We all need a means of feedback to not only make sure we are progressing in a correct fashion but also to ensure that we are efficient and avoid mountains of rework.

A critical aspect of feedback is ensuring that you have created communication feedback loops so that your team will not speculate on what you want and what is happening. It is very easy for the lack of direction to cause organizational noise that distracts and misleads the team.

Capacity

"We need more headcount." This is how capacity discussions often start. "No" is how they often end. We may or may not need more head count but we know there is a capacity issue. We are not able to keep up with demand or when we forecast for future work we can't see how it will be done. Capacity planning is easier to see if we are working with production lines and know the turn-around times and machine capabilities. It is more challenging when we have less defined processes.

We can rightly criticize leaders for asking us to squeeze one more thing in without more headcount or time. Of course we can't blame them when so often it works. We need to continuously look for ways to expand capacity. It can be extra help and it can be lots of other things. For me leverage is the key. Managers who manage efficiently within their resources can do a good job, leaders who widely leverage for extra resources can achieve much more.

Everyone works for me and I work for everyone

This little saying is one of my core guiding thoughts. First it reminds me that there are lots of people willing to help. This starts with anyone with a stake in my success and/or that I can help make successful. When you really think about it, that tends to be a really large group. Once I was invited to a large company for lunch with everyone who wanted to work for them for free arranged by a consulting firm. I think to our collective surprise, the cafeteria was full.

Leverage can be collaboration, partnering, and asking for help. It might be as simple as starting in our own teams and asking for their ideas. I assume that there isn't a need to start from zero on anything. Do an online search and leverage previous practice and models. There is always a way to get a head start. You may be surprised to find that capacity constraints are often self-imposed.

In my practice I have adopted a bias of trying to say "yes" first before I come up with all of the reasons for no. Even if I can't directly help, I can probably make a suggestion or a connection with someone who can. In organizations we can compete for resources or we can work together. Resources aren't "mine" they belong to the organization. Being open to sharing and supporting each other will lead to greater mutual success and support a foundation of flexibility for when it is needed.

Processes

Organizations run on processes. An important change readiness technique is to be diligent in updating and streamlining our processes. Good processes lead to consistency, efficiency and incorporate built-in flexibility. By maintaining a continuous improvement approach we maintain logical and reasonable effort. Work makes sense.

Processes like ships in the harbor pick up barnacles. On ships, these little crustaceans have to be periodically scraped off to cut down on drag. We have an ongoing need to keep our processes streamlined and relevant. Abraham Lincoln said, "Give me six hours to chop down a tree and I will spend the first four sharpening the axe." Process improvement keeps the axe for our work sharp.

Infrastructure

Infrastructure is a blanket term for the things we have to work with including our organizational structure, allocated budgets and head count, IT systems, and plant and equipment. Often it is seen as the barrier to change and improvement. With a focus on leverage and continuous improvement this is much less true. I prefer to think of infrastructure as the foundation for growth, it is the starting place, not the stopping point.

Connection

How is our sense of belonging? Are we a unified team or a band of individuals? Do we have weak bonds or strong bonds to the team and the organization? This element of connection and sense of belonging is a core element of culture. It can be cultivated and it should be managed. There are many kinds of glue that stick us together. We are bound together by comradery, shared achievement, mutual respect, gossip, shared dislike, and the experience of difficulty and trauma.

We want to be part of an effort that is valuable. We also want to be on a successful team. The trick is to promote belonging in our team and maintain our connection to the larger enterprise. Issues arise when we become too tribal and see our connection at too small a level. We need to practice being good at being the IT department, the Asia Pacific team, and part of the overall company.

One piece of advice that I have often given people planning their careers is to join an organization they believe in. It's the starting place for meaningful work and the precursor to being able to make a positive and productive connection. It is also really hard to stay connected to something you aren't proud of or don't believe in. Our actions either reinforce this value or call it into question.

Reputation

As leaders we are responsible for managing our collective reputation. We benefit from the good works of any member of our group, and can be damaged by the errors made by just one person. A strong reputation supports change readiness and the realization of value from change.

In new positons I have always started by gauging the reputation of the team. It may or may not be completely accurate but the perception of others does define the opportunity. In one case, I came into an organization where the team felt they were providing world class service and they actually knew much better than the management group what needed to be done. On the other hand senior management found them to be out of touch and wondered if it was even worth keeping the group. We had a major reputation issue.

Reputation maintenance and repair is active. It also has to have real value to be credible. There are two core contributors to creating positive reputations; doing important work, and broad visibility for achievement. We must maintain focus on important work and deliver the results. We must also share the limelight and include those who contributed to provide personal recognition and expand the overall group's reputation.

One of the best stories I can share goes back to the struggling team I mentioned earlier. By focusing on a major issue in the organization, determined effort and lots of team visibility we completely turned the reputation around. I knew that we had accomplished this when one day I was called by a President of a new business unit. He said that he needed someone to lead a similar function on his team. He told me, "I don't know who they are but I know they report to you, who do you suggest?"

Willingness

Willingness like the more tangible aspects of readiness is well worth our efforts to encourage and reward. Back in my Navy days I had a good friend who was a few years older named Dave. As you might imagine there were regularly details that no one was excited to do. When they asked for volunteers people would look at their shoes or up in the air. Not Dave. He would step forward and be the first to take on those jobs.

I observed that Dave regularly did this. He didn't complain or act like he was being put upon. I also started to observe that when there was something special to do, a reward, those often also went to Dave. I saw him after many years and told him that I tell this story, he said, "Yes, I still do that." Willingness was, and is, Dave's strategy for success.

Involvement

One of the most important things we can do to prepare for and manage change is get others involved. Involvement leads to action and action gives people a sense of control. Even in situations where we have little choice, starting to do things is the path to getting through change both practically and emotionally.

Being part of the process and engaging in action reduces the fear and speculation. Even small efforts are useful. We learn to be engaged by being invited to be involved. Of course there are times when changes need to be closely held for some period. When that is the case, we get others involved as soon as possible and have specific immediate actions for them to contribute.

We are responsible for managing the risk of decision making and for our teams learning to make good decisions and getting things done. We can't be overly cautious and hold onto everything ourselves becoming the bottleneck that restricts progress. In fact the more closely we hold onto efforts, plans and control, the less likely they are to succeed. Success comes from engaging others and letting them be part of the solution. There are rarely perfect ideas, even our own, and the little bit of inclusion goes a long way toward better implementation of solutions.

Trust

Trust is a central component in building readiness for change. We need to be trustworthy and cultivate trust in our teams. Being trustworthy doesn't mean that we always do what everyone wants or that there aren't difficult times ahead. It means that as a team we can rely on each other and know what to expect from our behavior. It means that we personally can be relied on to accomplish our tasks and be effective leaders.

A manager never has a bad day

As I stood in the back of a large first-line supervisor course I heard an older senior leader make this statement. I immediately thought, "Oh no he has gone senile." Everyone has a bad day. Managers can't be expected to be perfect. But I realized as he spoke what he meant. Leaders are the primary role models for teams to turn to for reassurance and guidance. We set the tone. Every day and in every action our trustworthiness is being judged. As leaders we demonstrate that we are capable of managing the risks and responsibility entrusted to us. Through our behavior we earn the willingness of others to follow our direction.

So how do you become trustworthy? Do you need to get everything right? No, but there are a few key things that should be consistent. The first is consistency itself. You regularly deliver and people know what to expect.

One of the ways to destroy personal and organizational credibility is complaining about your leaders with/or in front of your staff. It is fine to question and you have a responsibility to raise issues with those who can do something about it. If you assume the position of another victim to corporate process you have weakened the entire system and promoted learned helplessness.

I know, some of you are saying, "but they are wrong!" I'm sure in some instances that is correct, so are we. I'm not saying you become a mindless yes person, or ignore bad behavior. You have a responsibility to do your best to resolve issues and in some cases make very difficult decisions for the good of the organization. This means action not just criticism. Ask to ensure you understand.

It is a well-worn saying and still true, we have to walk our talk to earn trust. We have all seen credibility killed when leaders can't follow their own rules and expectations. A simple test for us to gauge whether we should take an action is to ask if we would approve of our reports or other managers doing it. If not, don't do it.

I have a simple rule for myself which is - follow the rules. For some people they think that this means being inflexible. Actually what this means is become predictable and reliable. I'm always happy to appeal to the persons and systems in place for making exceptions. At the same time I avoid making exceptions that exceed my authority. Those times where managers take it upon themselves to bend the rules can lead to a culture of unethical behavior and perceptions of favoritism.

We all naturally gravitate to some people and maybe want to avoid others. This is not a luxury we have in organizations. We need to practice organizational forgiveness. Talking about forgiveness might seem odd for a leadership discussion but it is a core aspect of trust. Essentially we need to be able to get over things, our mistakes and those of others.

This doesn't mean we limit accountability. We just don't vilify a person for errors. When we question the basic self-worth of a person we are destroying confidence and creating the potential for a downward spiral. In reality, if behavior is so egregious that we have lost trust in someone our responsibility is to remove them from the organization. If not, our responsibility is to coach and help them improve, provide clear expectations, and help get them back on-track.

Just as we can't over-do-it on our response to errors, we also can't ignore or downplay issues. A trap some managers fall into is being sympathetic instead of empathetic. It isn't parsing terms. When we are empathetic we understand and can see through another's perspective. When we are sympathetic we feel sorry for them and may stray from appropriate behaviors.

Even when negative management actions are taken, if we have established that we are trustworthy, our teams will be able to rebound more quickly. They will know through our pattern of behavior that we are supporting organizational and individual success and that our actions are not motivated by favoritism or caprice. They will understand that we take our responsibilities seriously and try our best to live up to an appropriate standard.

A leader's primary job is in achieving organizational results in a fashion that is consistent with organizational values and expectations. All teams want to win. Being on a winning team is both satisfying and motivating. If we want to establish a positive virtual spiral, we need to win and do so in a way we are proud of and can share. Leaders who are only in it for themselves quickly lose credibility. The way we win trust, and our personal rewards, is to ensure organizational and individual wins for our team and our partners and do it as often as possible.

Is all change valuable?
The Three things

In change workshops I ask participants "Is all change valuable?" Some say yes, others no and then we generally get to, "It depends." It depends on if you have learned anything from it. I believe that in fact all change is valuable and the road to learning from it really only includes three things.

Sometimes when a person comes to a workshop they are hoping to learn some magic that will make life and change easier. In fact there are some ideas and models here that do just that. There may also be an awareness of how important your role is and what great responsibility leadership can be so that actually learning more has made it harder. Don't worry you are up to the task.

Understanding starts with knowledge. Wisdom comes from understanding and practice. The good news here is that you get to practice constantly. Life is just set up that way and work is no different. Even in the most mundane and repetitive experiences there are opportunities to learn. Those opportunities are described by three areas or domains if you like, where you can learn and practice. You can use change to learn about: Yourself, Others and Your Craft.

Some people think that every day they go to a factory or an office and give up a pound of flesh for their paycheck. It is a bad trade and they feel abused. Consider instead that when you go to work they are paying you to learn, to add to your personal human capital and marketability. The choice is yours and depends on how you exploit the learning available in any environment.

Learning about our craft is the most typical area for our learning. If we are accountants we learn about financial transactions and supporting systems. If we are operations manager we learn about turnaround time, plant layout and quality control. If we are senior leaders we learn about strategy, Board relationships and working with the press.

Learning about other people is not just learning about personality profiles and going to soft skills classes. All work is social and all organizations are political. You may be tempted to recoil from the "political" term. Don't take that negatively. It means that all of us have agendas and desires. Those compete and cooperate in social settings.

The aspects of learning about others are twofold. We learn about individuals, what motivates them, how to deal with personal conflict, and how to help them be successful. We also learn about teams and groups and the structures that enable performance and those that inhibit success.

I maintain that everyone is uniquely the same. We share a lot of common needs and personal psychology. At the same time we are at different places in life, face different challenges outside of work, come from different backgrounds, and have different cultural influences and beliefs. One caution here - Do not be tempted to become an amateur psychologist. I try to give great latitude for individuality within the guardrails of being productive and generally getting along. I don't expect anyone to be perfect. We are all learning.

The last category is the most important. Learning about ourselves. Some people spend a great deal of focus here. Some are overly self-critical and others appear to be oblivious to their impacts on others. Human beings all think they are right. This is necessary for us to function. As leaders we need to be confident and make calls. We also need to maintain a degree of self-reflection and humility.

Emotional intelligence has developed over millennia to help protect and guide us. When our emotions tell us that someone is upset these are important signals and warnings. Practicing listening to our emotions doesn't mean becoming driven by whim or becoming emotionally manipulative. It is using all of our senses and faculties to understand situations and guide our responses. This is particularly useful in ethical considerations. If it feels wrong, it probably is.

One of the great paradoxes in life, and management, is the failure to make a choice, is a choice. We can guide our practice of leadership by the unseen patterns we have picked up from parents, authority figures and former bosses. We can instinctively react to situations driven by our desires and fears, unconsciously extending our emotional responses as we try to provide motivation and direction. We must become students of change and ourselves. What we learn is what we will use to frame situations and motivate and guide others.

Change readiness leads to a higher degree of competence (knowing how) and confidence (knowing I/we can). This is what we create to build our resilience to weather the storms and to achieve our goals. We practice on the easy days to be ready for the great challenges. We find the new and renew ourselves and others.

This is how we make change valuable. We leverage it. Learn from it. Practice, make mistakes and correct. There is a lot to learn to create change readiness. We have the time if we use the time we have to do it. The efficiency is that it is constant and if we decide to be attentive the lessons will be all around us. Expertise requires practice. Let's embrace that as long as we are here, we will be practicing change and building our expertise.

*If you accept the challenge
of leadership it will become
your life's work*

Chapter Four
Intention

Intention results in two outcomes –

Achieving the goals that we believe will lead to success, and **becoming** who we want to be along the way.

Intention is the power to create direction. It is active and it can be shared. It is the source of motivation and the beginning of agendas and plans. Intention describes the way and the destination. In every action we take, we can reinforce our intentions or violate them. Intention can be a powerful tool to bring teams and organizations together or a guessing game that creates fear and doubt.

Intention is related to the readiness elements we discussed previously. It identifies priorities and expectation which are communicated and reinforced maintaining clarity. It also motivates thus laying the foundation for involvement, willingness and ultimately trust. Shared Intention enables us to be on the same page and create the basis for a positive and productive culture. When we know that our leaders have good intentions it is much easier to follow them into the unknown.

Scalpel or Chainsaw?

This may seem like an odd question but consider that both of these tools can be effective in accomplishing an amputation. One is considerably more messy. We have all experienced change by brute force and seen it work. The choice we make with our change intentions is to achieve a goal and maintain a set of behaviors. It is more than just getting this change done. It is about the long game of getting lots of changes done and creating an organization that is flexible and nimble because it practices change in a consistent and trustworthy fashion.

The other aspect of our change approach implied by this question is that we avoid collateral damage. If we need big change, we do big change. If it needs to be quick and has negatively viewed results we still do it. However, we lead change; we don't create an impression that it leads us. One of the most important things for us to do is to create a sense of control for the organization and for individuals. We don't become frantic; we maintain our values as we advance toward our goals. A sense of control doesn't mean that we control everything. This is an important distinction. Bad things happen in life and organizations. The sense of control comes when we start to do something about it.

Picking our battles

Do we need to cultivate and practice change readiness constantly – yes. Do we need to manage all changes – no! In some cases if we leave things alone they work out on their own. If it isn't important and can't be improved now then it is not a good candidate for concerted effort.

A hazard with any action is unintended consequences. We might get what we want and we will get others things too. So we start to put a new system in place and soon discover that the unknown legacy integrations blow our timeline. We can't predict the future and our experience tells us that unforeseen things happen in the wake of our efforts.

We also realize that some problems just can't be solved - yet. We may decide to be on the leading edge of change for new innovations or wait until the cost has gone down and the details figured out. Doing nothing is sometimes the best choice for the situation or for the time being.

Some issues don't ever get solved; they're just conditions that come with the management territory. Tasks like taking care of today while preparing for tomorrow can create conflict but both are important so we don't choose between one or the other, we must do both.

One way to choose the important areas we need to support with dedicated change effort is to determine if there is high:

- Risk
- Complexity
- Novelty
- Scope/scale
- Cost, or
- Potential Value

The other changes that we want to routinely pursue are those that are still important and really easy to make and/or have minor impacts. The low-risk, low-cost and still worthwhile things that are often obvious. Obvious, however, is in the eye of the beholder. So another aspect of picking our battles is determining what we are fighting and if we have a shared perception of the threat (motivation to change), particularly among the senior leadership team and the project or task group.

It is better to do nothing, than be busy doing nothing
loa Tsu

Dragons, Elephants or Puppies?

I like to think about areas for possible change activities as represented by three animals; Dragons, Elephants, or Puppies. This model nicely describes priority and some hazards associated with choosing actions based on the perception of the threat.

Dragons are the preferred change threats. They are dangerous and breathe fire. Most people recognize them and you get famous if you are a dragon slayer. Stories are written and songs sung about the heroic battles waged and won. Those heroic times we beat the impending doom, got the miracle account, or made the pivot just in time.

I advise new leaders to look for dragons. Even tiny little ones that can be held between two fingers. Slaying dragons builds momentum, and credibility. We are seen as people who can get things done and step up when needed. Great change leaders need the visibility and recognition of dragon slayers.

There are problems, however, with being the King or Queen's favorite knight. There is lots of competition for a seat at the round table. Dragon slaying is also addictive and it might even cause us to start seeing dragons where they aren't. We might be tempted to expect constant heroic behavior. So we have to be cautious.

Dragon slayers get lots of attention. The focus on individual effort can make it look like, "it's all about me." A conundrum is that while we need personal success, we also need to be team players. An antidote to this affliction is to have several dragon slayers who get to take turns or better yet lead the mob that gets the dragon.

I'm sure you have heard the saying, "The elephant in the room." We all know of those situations or issues that everyone knows about and no one does anything about. These can be just as big a threat as dragons but much harder and less popular to battle.

A central problem with elephants is that they have become the convenient excuse for inaction. For any number of reasons, they have become a protected species. Everyone knows about them and they all accept that nothing will be done. So everyone has a good excuse, we all nod knowingly but most people are happy to join the status quo.

The best strategy with these beasts is to try to get others to see them as the dragons that are behind the lovable facade. It won't be easy. Sometimes you will have to face them anyway and while these battles are organizationally important, you will have limited support for your efforts. It will be less fun and heroic. Don't expect a parade and ensure that at least the key sponsors like your senior leadership or the Board have your back.

Remember that while dragons are solitary beings, elephants are social animals. There are always social issues that come with elephants. Elephant hunting exposes the tacit acceptance of a problem by a group and the failure of specific individuals to do anything. Consider extra care and efforts at concurrent social interventions like more involvement, shared effort and group alignment.

No one likes people who kill puppies. You might be experiencing waves of revulsion just by the suggestion. Puppies are cute and cuddly and we just love them. I'm sorry but it illustrates an important point. Puppies are those pet projects and protected people and processes that leaders keep around. We dutifully clean up after them but they never quit making messes or stop chewing things up like our resources.

Most puppies belong to powerful people. They might be little handbag dogs that you see on the plane or aggressive exotic pit bulls. No matter what, they are like the third rail on the subway, potentially lethal if you touch them.

Of course some people have great perceptual clarity and they see little green wings on these puppies and those canine teeth are really sharp and curved backwards. Yes, they can be, or can grow into, dragons.

The hazard for puppy owners is at some point the perception of their uselessness becomes general. It seems like everyone sees the folly of their pet choices but them. Now we have the classic "Emperor has no clothes" story. The people all fawn on the leader's pet and talk about how beautiful they are but in reality we know that they are not and the leader pays a price in credibility for the choice to keep them.

So like elephants you need to change the perception of the puppy owners in order to deal with the issues. Don't expect this one to be easy. Remember that you are dealing with bonds of affection and not logic. Unfortunately, sometimes you just have to wait until they have made a big enough mess or help to create a situation where it is more obvious. Here are a few suggestions to help when you have fights that are not easy or popular:

1.) Take others with you, always a good suggestion.

2.) Maintain a close connection with someone who has a clear vison of organizational reality who can help maintain your perspective.

3.) Remember we battle problems and change; we don't fight with each other. Avoid circling the wagons and then shooting inside.

A final point about picking battles. Fighting in organizations isn't fair. Now I don't mean actual fighting or even action that might be perceived as aggression at all. But there are lots of times when people get wounded at least metaphorically. The scar that forms from these wounds is called disillusionment. Now I like to think that personally I'm so disillusioned that there is nowhere to go but to be optimistic. Believe me that is the result of lots of practice.

Life gives us lots of disillusionment. It starts when we are children and learn that are parents really don't know everything and then creeps into most of our experiences when we learn that people don't always meet our high expectations or preconceived beliefs. At work we see people get promoted because they are friends, or lucky or any number of other reasons that make us say, "I can't believe they promoted that idiot over me." It hurts.

My advice is to congratulate people on their good fortune and take care of yourself. Don't allow the pain to make you bitter and ineffective. Look for the learning in the situation. Have you been marginalized? Was it just bad luck because the favorite child came back to the business? Is there a glass/concrete/poison gas ceiling that is the limit your potential progression? Try to be realistic. Sometimes we just need to be patient. Our turn is going to come.

However, if you are blocked from contributing fully and getting what you deserve by The CEO who isn't going anywhere it may be time to weigh your choices. We always have choices. I like to think that the root of self-empowerment is that we know we can make a choice when we like. It is our life. We have limited time to do what we want and be who we want to be. Work is only an enabler. No place or job is the only place our dreams can come true.

Changes we are responsible for will also result in negative impacts for the people we lead and care about. The choice we have at these points is to double down on our integrity, empathy and honesty. I have seen managers vilify employees when they have to give layoff notices. It is a convenient emotional trick they use to sooth themselves, acting like the action was personally deserved. The problem with this approach is that it is dishonest and the behavior will erode trust with other employees and make it worse for effected people.

The hardest part of all of this is usually it doesn't really have anything to do with you or them at all. The layoff comes and you just happen to be in the impacted department. It is hard to do but don't take life too personally. We do what we can, as best we can. Start by using the change magic of taking control of your own future by establishing an intention to do your best and try to remember to also always strive to be who you want to be.

Appreciating Resistance

It may sound a little odd but as we work with change we need to appreciate resistance to our efforts. In most discussions in change courses and books resistance is described as those inevitable things people do to reduce our effectiveness and slow our progress because they don't want to do what we want them to.

We will go over that kind of behavior shortly but first let's understand the value of resistance and resistors. Resistance informs, prepares and protects us during change. It makes sure that we make sure and if we pay attention we will use it to the collective advantage of our organizations and ourselves as leaders.

Resistance is a natural expression. Sometimes of concern, sometimes of frustration and often of a desire to help ensure that we will be as OK as possible and not make a mess of things. Our response to resistance tells people a lot about us personally and as leaders. Our response can reassure and connect or show impatience and disrespect. It can erode the trust others place in us if we ignore information and the need to modify our plans. Our teams will lose some of the willingness for readiness if we violate the trust between us.

I believe that in fact most resistance is created by mangers through poor change leadership. We get impatient and don't remember all the initial questions we ourselves may have had when starting to plan initiatives as we become tired of describing it yet again. We need to remain willing to share as much as we can as often as we can and be as honest as we can. Sometimes we don't know all of the details and it's fine to tell people that. If we have demonstrated that we are reliable in our efforts, we will be trusted as things come together.

If we act aggressively and through our language, demeanor, and/or tone appear to be attacking people we should expect for them to respond by defensiveness or a boomerang attack. We can always be assertive, we never need attack any of our colleagues especially our reports. Attacks demonstrate lack of control, care and empathy. Of course we all can get angry and that is OK, we must remember that we are always modeling what we expect and setting the tone.

Resistance is really useful if it keeps us from making a major mistake. No one is perfect and generally the more senior we get, the less in touch with the daily realities of the work. We need to leave space for adjustment in our grand plans by those who know. We also need to save a little space no matter what for some involvement and to maintain the sense of control others need.

Another very useful aspect of resistance is that it reveals how people are making sense of things. It helps us know where to start in guiding them to understanding and clarity of our intentions and how to be part of helping to support them. Resistance is also a barometer of commitment telling us how strong our connections are and where those need to be shored up.

Once a direct report started screaming at me in front of the members of the team they led. I didn't feel physically threatened or think anyone else was at risk so I told them to go home and see me in the morning. I knew a couple of things. There was a great deal of stress, many long hours and the behavior was uncharacteristic. It was a break and a mistake. I did prepare a formal written disciple memo and explained that it couldn't happen again and said that I and others were there to help. I was later actually able to promote them. It was an isolated incident for a very talented person.

My advice is to look at resistance through these lenses first. To ask ourselves what part we have played in creating it and how we can leverage it to accomplish our goals. I will also admit that there are going to be times when a person's reaction to change is outside of the useful range. That is often temporary and we need to deal with it appropriately ensuring we follow the rules and understand the person and situation.

Bring Me a Rock

The last reminder about intention is contained in a useful story I learned at work several years ago. Bring me a rock is a frustrating game leaders play. They will say, "Bring me a rock." The subordinate dutifully goes out and gets a rock and brings it back to the manager's office. The manager inspects the rock and says, "No, I meant a big rock." The subordinate now, slightly frustrated goes and gets a big rock. When she brings it back the manager says, "No, I meant a red rock, try again." So she goes and gets a red rock and brings it back. The manager says, 'You know, that first one was just fine."

I imagine we have all played this game where leaders provide so little guidance that we have no real idea what they are trying to accomplish. It is as if the little bit of effort for them to create clear expectations is too much trouble but all of the rework and stress further down in the organization is no big deal.

A related game is "Don't bring me problems, bring me solutions." This starts out as a well-intentioned effort to empower people but more often ends in frustration and a barrier between leaders and reports. If all they can see is the problem, help by engaging in some joint problem solving and work together to define the next step.

Chapter Five
Inspiration

The purpose of management is to accomplish organizational goals. In management we tell people what to do, assign them goals, organize their time, and give them rules for process and behavior. In effect, we make them do things. We have organizational authority and power by virtue of our positons and employees agree to submit to this authority as a condition of employment. Sounds a bit harsh when I put it like this doesn't it?

We need to start by removing some possible illusions. One is that everyone comes to work to express themselves in a creative activity that they have devoted their lives to having the opportunity to do. Another is that work should always be rewarding. The third illusion is that there is a requirement for people to be motivated beyond the basic agreements defined by the expectations for competent and productive effort. The final illusion for this discussion is that everyone should like what they are doing and like us.

In one of my first management jobs I was a production manager in a small factory. I had been in supervisory roles and had taken management courses in College. I was familiar with theory X and theory Y, and wanted to be a theory Y leader.

Theory X is also called scientific management. It is the great innovation of the early 20th century championed by Fredrick Taylor. It includes concepts like time and motion studies, task and job efficiency standards, systematic approaches to processes and the division of labor into highly efficient tasks. It is still widely practiced and it is often vilified as dehumanizing. The employee is a cog in the great machine with mind numbing work and little control.

In the period following World War II, a revolution in management thinking occurred, called humanism. Humanism is the basis for theory Y. It is about empowerment and choice. It is in large based on a positive psychology reflecting the significant gains made by that field and our understanding about meaning, motivation and self-realization. We lead because we love people and want to help them become self-actualized through work. We are servant leaders and enablers of performance vs ogres who demand effort.

In my desire to be a good theory Y leader I practiced treating employees with respect. I attempted to empower them to make decisions on their own. I generally described outcomes and let them determine the means to accomplish tasks. Occasionally I even made product on the line, the really helpful supervisor. The productivity of the team skyrocketed. People seemed happy and my boss was very happy.

One day I was walking through an area I managed and an employee called me over to her bench. She said, "You are the worst manager I have ever had." She also said, "I'm not paid enough to think, you are supposed to tell me what to do." As you can imagine I was shocked and wounded. Didn't she understand that I was treating her like I would like to be treated, that my management approach was a positive expression of my deepest values?

So I went to speak with the wise old plant superintendent for some advice. I told him the story and he said, "Fire her, there's a line out the door of people wanting to work here." So that didn't sound quite right, not what I was expecting. Surely I didn't have to do that.

As I thought about it, I realized that she was right. I wanted to be Theory Y as a manager but she was a Theory X employee. In her case I did need to give her more direction. After all, my job was to meet production quotas, not run social experiments. I am convinced that all managers do run experiments, we just don't think in those terms. I also realized that I was still a Theory X manager in that I expected people to get things done; I was just going about it in a more positive fashion. As far as I knew maybe there were others who would like to be less empowered. I hadn't asked anyone what they wanted. So I did. Major rookie mistake.

I called everyone to the conference room and I asked them what was wrong and then listened for two hours, on overtime, to problem after problem that I was not able to solve. It turned out that in fact no one seemed happy. They worked there because there were only two places in town with medical benefits and decent pay. It wasn't bad but I think everyone would have been OK with staying home and amusing themselves in their own ways.

Going back to the illusions mentioned earlier. While I love work and the challenge of solving the myriad of problems that come with leadership, not everyone shares my point of view. Sometimes, even for me, work is just an unpleasant slog through something we would rather not do. It's not fun, interesting or entertaining. I have developed a simple way to tell the difference between work and entertainment. Entertainment is almost all fun, I pay for it. Work can be fun but often isn't, I get paid for that.

I also have learned over time that I can't expect, or make, people like me. I do my best but that is their right and as long as they hold up their part of the productivity bargain they get to think of me as they will. I also don't take it personally. I think it is a true expression of my respect for them that I avoid judging people for things that don't matter. More about this later.

The other side of this as I've said before is that I'm not in leadership to make people happy either. I certainly don't try to actively make everyone unhappy but I don't accept that as an expectation for my performance. This is a really hard area for lots of managers and a prerequisite bias to abandon. It really is a fool's errand. Most of us have periods where we have no idea what we want or what will really make us happy. Trying to be all seeing in this area is not a good management job requirement.

In workshops when I say things like this I can see people cringe and I know that not every participant is open to agreeing to the point of view. They are like the younger version of me in the factory stuck in a preferred style where not only did I want people to do things but I also expected them to be happy about it, even if they preferred not to be. If you think about it, what an overstep of my authority.

It was really just all about me but sugar coated. I wanted to bask in their admiration of my superior leadership skills, to be good and popular. They just wanted a check. Now to finish that story, I didn't fundamentally change my approach. I had significantly increased productivity and that was the bottom line. The complaining employee eventually quit even with more direction. It just wasn't what she wanted to do. I did learn an important lesson, and I appreciate her help in teaching me.

I can hear you now saying something like, "Hey didn't the title of this book have something to do with inspiring change?" Yes and I think it is the preferred path. Let's take a look at a few definitions:

Motivate
Make somebody willing: to make somebody feel enthusiastic, interested, and committed to something. Cause somebody's behavior

Coerce
Force somebody: to make somebody do something against his or her will by using force or threats

Inspire
Stimulate somebody to do something: to encourage somebody to greater effort, enthusiasm, or creativity

Source: Bing Dictionary

Let's revisit a few things. As leaders we are responsible for achieving goals, our primary task is to get things done. Sometimes our team members will want to get them done too in an enthusiastic fashion and sometimes not. As a leader we are also responsible for motivating them to complete the tasks. It is funny when we look at the definition of motivation it starts with "Make Somebody." We have two general ways to do this motivating, coercion and Inspiration. In reality we do both when needed and more often by our own choice.

I don't know about you but I sure would prefer to be inspired than coerced. It sounds more agreeable. There may, however, be a good argument made that in fact all management is inherently coercion because we are making people do things they otherwise would not do. Through rewards and punishments and a wide range of means we manipulate them into doing our will.

There is another red herring word – manipulate. That sounds really bad doesn't it? Let's look at it in a little more clinical sense. In behavioral modification we motivate individuals through the manipulation of positive and negative reinforcement. Yes that's what we do. We get them to do something with carrots and sticks. This is a really big deal. When we realize that a core aspect of our work in motivating people is manipulating their behavior we should be very careful and know what we are doing.

So back to choice. We get to pick carrots and sticks. We know that people respond to different motivators and we know that things we might call negative also work. But when we go back to our definitions there is an important difference that isn't just about our preferred values, it is about how much value we create – our primary task. If we re-read coerce and inspire we see that inspiration results in greater productivity. Is this a trick like the soldiers in Stone Soup? Well, yes and no.

Choosing to be inspirational even when we are being coercive is our choice. It is not making everyone happy but it is doing the best we can at making the situation as valuable and positive for everyone as possible and exceeding our productivity expectations. Winning and winning in the best ways possible.

When I ask people to think of a leader who inspired change they often think of great leaders like Gandhi, Kennedy, or other political or movement leaders. Maybe they think of family members, their Dad or Grandmother or an Uncle. They also think of the good bosses they have reported to previously. Some of these leaders were inspirational through charisma, others through a loving approach to humanity, or a great cause, or even a good story.

Let's look at a contrast between out motivators again. Some of the many ways to coerce or inspire:

A few coercive techniques –

Fear, because I said so, moral superiority, positional authority, engendering hatred, physical force, exclusion from a group/isolation, anger, attack, giving no choice, negative peer pressure, berating, creating uncertainty, threat, loss of status or benefit, brow beating, extortion, hostage taking, bullying, yelling and screaming, and all forms of violence.

As you look at the list it might occur to you that you have done some or even many of them in your relationship and as a leader. We seem to particularly favor these approaches when the time is short and the risk is high and when what we are trying to do is highly unpopular. We also do these a lot with children and others who we think can't decide for themselves. It's really pretty common human behavior and it can be natural and easy. It also works. Let's now look at some inspirational techniques.

A few inspirational techniques –

Love, vision, trust, achievement, contribution, empathy, a grand cause, belief in others, shared sacrifice, mutual interest, a great story, excitement, belonging, positive peer pressure, adventure, safety, innovation, affiliation, a higher good, positive self-image, respect, involvement, listening, providing choices, understanding, forgiveness, openness.

I think there is no question that most of us would pick the inspirational techniques if we had the choice. This is the part of intention where we get to choose being who we want to be. There may still be times where we slip into coercion, and as pointed out as long as we are using anything to make someone do something, positive or negative, it is a coercive practice at its root. But remember inspiration works too and it works better.

Inspiration tends to create more of what we want with less pain, collateral damage or conflict in the process. If you look at the inspirational techniques list I know you see some that you are already good at, that you do naturally. These are your leadership talents and gifts. You don't need to be the most outgoing and charismatic person to be a good leader. A thoughtful person who is a good listener is also inspirational. Someone who believes in us is one of the most inspiring leaders.

The process of finding your best inspirational techniques is a journey of self-discovery. It requires reflection and practice. Think about it as your own leadership intention. What do you want to achieve and who do you want to be? That will give you a head start. What you value, you aspire to be. Being aspirational and authentic means trying to be your best self while you accomplish your goals.

The first, and most important step, is to choose to try. Give yourself the permission to be your inspirational self and try it out. Make some mistakes and find some things that work and really feel right for you. Others help. Listen to what you are complemented on. It might not be in a leadership context but you have been hearing these things your entire life. I have heard many times that I'm a good listener, and a calming presence, and can tell a good story. These are gifts that I love to share and that I have found work to inspire performance.

Alternative sources of power

Power is the energy to get things done. We may also attach negative connotations to power so let's take another look and maybe a different perspective. If motivating people is making them willing, coercion is making them do it and inspiring is stimulating them to do more, then it appears that we are using power in all cases. We might also recognize that like before we prefer the kind of power that stimulates us vs makes us. So how is inspiration powerful?

Two year olds are right when they get frustrated with their parents telling them, "Because I said so." We don't like that answer any more as adults. We also don't like, "Because I'm the boss." Power used to create a real or implied threat is natural to resist. We are going to jump on the fight or flight express when we face these situations. It is the natural and most likely response. So this energy, this power, is the application of brute force, sometimes subtle and sometimes pure personal intimidation. No wonder people are afraid of powerful people. We have learned to be careful.

The energy from coercion does not get multiplied in a complementary fashion. It gets opposed and hopefully diffused as we try to protect ourselves. The power from inspiration is different. It is exponential, our efforts get multiplied by a ready and aligned team.

Maybe it's possible that being coercive all day really drains a leader's personal power. Being a jerk can really take it out of you. Being inspirational reenergizes us as well as those we lead. Another significant advantage for the choice of options. It is more efficient, productive, and good for us too.

A few simple examples of the power of inspiration. How do you feel when your leader asks for your opinion or advice? Maybe in a meeting when someone says, "good idea." Or even more simply, you are told a sincere, "Thank you." At one point I realized that we all crave validation and we are stingy with giving it. Why? Are we afraid that we will lose our power if we are polite human beings? I know that answer is no. I also know that these seemingly minor actions are inspirational motivators that create change readiness and will pay off when the going gets tough.

I know that you are at least intrigued by inspirational leadership because you have invested your time in reading this book. Maybe you wondered how you could do it. We tend to think of larger than life persons when we think inspiration. Where do you start? The good news is it is easier than we might think. Start with a few little things. Be authentically inspirational on a small scale. It's a good start and a good ongoing practice. In every interaction you have the power to motivate or discourage, use your power wisely.

All the cool kids are doing it

One of my favorite interventions (leadership tools) is positive peer pressure. We are social beings and in all social groups we create norms and monitor the behavior of others. We always do it, everywhere. Remember back in the awkward days of adolescence how important it was to fit in? We still want to be part of the group that has influence with the important people at work. One of the worst things for us is to be isolated from the mainstream. We will even start to accept things we don't agree or believe in if there is enough social momentum.

So we know that peer pressure in the extreme is the dangerous mob mentality. Exclusion is a terrible thing to do to anyone. I consider a range of peer pressure elements to be clearly in the coercive camp; group bullying, discrimination based on anything, not inviting people to lunch when the group goes, and not sharing information. Another behavior that can get out of hand is humor. We all enjoy a laugh but we need to make sure we aren't laughing at others and especially not in groups.

I was teaching a class once and there was a young woman who sat in the back and never said anything. One day she responded to a question with an answer that was off track and actually funny. I stifled the laugh reaction and no one else laughed either. If I had laughed I know that everyone else would have.

The damage that could have done would have negated anything positive she got from the class. The rule of thumb is that making fun of ourselves is generally OK, making fun of other should be limited to very close groups of old friends and even then done very carefully.

Creating positive peer pressure is easier than it sounds. By consistently rewarding what we want with an inspirational gift (think thank you or other simple validation) in public we will create a virtuous cycle. Now like everything we do we can't be obvious manipulators for devious ends, that puts us back in the coercive camp. Genuine expression not only energizes it also reinforce expectations and leads to clarity. A secret we shared earlier is don't do things by yourself. Always involve and leverage others. It gets more done and creates a better environment. Take the responsibility and share the opportunity.

You may need to deal with a negative energy source competing for control of your teams. A person who is influential in the group that has become negative or outright counterproductive. Remember that your power is not diminished by others. Don't allow an attack to throw you off. It is natural to be taken aback when it happens but don't respond in-kind or become defensive. A good approach to get them back on track is to reinforce expectations and remind them in clear terms.

Do not ignore poor behavior. Remember it is contagious. Practice inspirational feedback and correction. Acknowledge the issue, listen to the point, accommodate points if they are relevant good ideas, reinforce that value the person brings, and communicate that you expect that they continue. You must be diligent in this effort as employee performance and behavior issues quickly escalate to elephants in the room if ignored and will massively reduce your credibility.

Inspirational behavior in escalating performance issues is grounded in consistency, respect and adherence to organizational values and processes. This doesn't mean you can't be flexible when warranted. Most organizations have paths for legitimate appeal. As a leader your primary responsibility is to accomplishing the goals of the organization and it is a slippery slope to engage in personalized negotiations. In the end that only leads to lost trust when you are not consistent or predictable.

When I was a child I had the opportunity to go to Boy's Club camp every summer. The Director was a wonderful inspiring man. He used to say when we misbehaved, "Your parents are showing." As leaders, we are not parents but consider that there is truth to the statement, "Your leader is showing" in demonstrations of group norms and behavior.

Everyone is watching

Everything counts. Don't get paranoid but people are watching. Like it or not, as leaders we are role models in all situations at all times. We don't get to turn it off and be part of the group. We can be in the group and enjoy everyone's company, but we can't stop being the boss. Inconsistencies in our behavior can damage our ability to get things done. When we make mistakes it is also very important to work on recovering as soon as possible. In these instances we demonstrate what we expect when this happens to others. Admitting when we have been wrong is also inspirational. We are being open and honest.

No one can get it perfectly right all the time. The upside of everyone watching is that we have constant opportunities to be influential. This may seem like a heavy burden. Actually if you practice it becomes second nature. You can demonstrate setting expectations, building trust and creating a positive environment just by being yourself.

In the end, the consistent use of inspirational behavior is the best response to critical events whether they are organizational changes or personal issues. Practice every day and while you will continue to get difficult issues to deal with, you will be better and better prepared.

Chapter Six
Approach

The change toolbox

How do we get change done? We know from our previous discussion that it is a constant process. It flows by us all day and we intervene with an occasional decision, choice or direction. Think about all of the seemingly minor decisions you make. While they may not seem to be a big deal, they add up to where you are going.

This daily activity on small things and bigger issues is in effect practicing good judgment. Good judgment is the means and measure of our effort to achieve our intentions. We say someone has good judgement when they accomplish goals in a fashion that we expect. The goals are accomplished through three related managerial competencies; change leadership, project management, and proficiency with change tools.

The focus of this book is change leadership and to get the big picture we will briefly explore the other aspects. They are all areas for study by themselves and should be part of any manager's development both in formal education and training and guided mentoring and practice.

Good Project Management is Good Change Management

The good news about large scale change management is that it can be systematically accomplished through the process of project management. The degree of formality in using project management depends on things like complexity and cost. The more risky, broad in impact and potentially valuable, the more need for formal project management.

The elements of change readiness like creating clear intentions and inspirational motivation always fit and create more efficiency and effectiveness in project management. Plans at any level from strategic goals and initiatives to daily direction are no more than change roadmaps. In essence project management on any scale is the step-by-step action plans to accomplish those desired changes.

Desired change is typically realized through a set of common change tools that can be summarized as; technology, process, and organization. They tend to be linked such that a shift in one also impacts the others and all of them are dependent on people in the end in order to work.

Technology

Technology solutions are a favorite means of change. Much of what we do now is embedded in technology. Software packages, ERP systems, and automation are logical, mostly pre-defined, and come with known desired outcomes. We can benefit from implementing a known system that has been proved in other environments reducing the challenge and cost. Even with configurable systems, a major advantage of technology based change is its usually well-defined path, choices and structure.

There is no question that new systems come with new threats and unknown risks. Technology is often associated with job loss and deskilling. At the same time the power to globally connect, make sense of our patterns of activity and communicate have massively increased. Like everything, good and bad.

We rarely are concerned about the ability of people to use computers, a common major issue in adoptions just a few years ago. The ability to participate and engage in technological change has also grown exponentially as the use of apps and self-created personal support IT systems flourish. We may not think of it in this way but we don't give a second thought to building our own support systems by choosing our mobile devices apps, favorite social networking tools and productivity enhancers.

As leaders this foundation of broad understanding, adoption and familiarity provides us with a massive head-start in further technology enhancements. We are used to it. The other comforting aspect of this is that the basics still apply. The components of clear intentions, systematic planning and inspirational motivation still work.

In fact, expanding technology choices have also increased our inspirational options. More persons can be involved through distributed engagement. The world continues to shrink and we can communicate on a more personal level with almost anyone in the world anytime and we have much more in common by the virtual environments that have become common space for human experience. Remember too that there are many low technology choices that are not difficult or expensive that can also be highly effective like thank you notes, photos, and Lean inspired visual management tools.

As leaders we need to know what technological solutions can expand our productivity and help us accelerate reaching our goals. We also can take advantage of technology to accelerate the being who we want to be aspect of our intentions. Messaging can be enhanced and multiplied increasing clarity. We can solicit ideas promoting involvement and a sense of control more readily, understand and address concerns, and provide immediate and broad visibility and appreciation to contributors.

Process

"How do we do that?" The answer is a process. Most organizations have these rules and best practices in every nook and cranny. They emerge because something is important enough, complex enough, or risky enough to make sure we do it in a certain prescribed way. Processes get formalized in workflows, standard operating procedures, guidelines, rules, policies, and protocols. Informal processes emerge where we develop habits for our work that we always use but aren't somewhere in writing or embedded in a system.

All processes need to be periodically reviewed to ensure ongoing alignment with the upstream inputs and the needs of downstream systems that depend on them. We have lots of good tools for process improvement from flowcharting to Lean and Six Sigma methods. Both process definition and process improvement provide natural inspirational change opportunities and great team involvement.

You might be inclined to think, "Wow that stuff is boring and tedious and almost no one gets excited about processes." This may be true. It can be a lot of work to get a good definition of process flow. Lots of organizational lines can be crossed, there can be many owners and influencers and there's almost always many ways to do anything. So where is the inspirational part?

Processes are inherently logical. They are like a puzzle where we have all the parts, we just need to see the picture and make the connections. This of course can be complex and at the same time can be a strong motivator when we can provide clarity of the outcome and operating conditions we want. It can also be fun.

If we change our point of view from tedious conference room debates and endless confusing details to identifying tamable dragons we start to see possibilities. We can distribute leadership, recognize lots of good ideas, involve and give people a sense of control. We all know that those closest to the work also likely know how to do it better and want to be included in making that happen. We can leverage that for successful completion of the change and inspire engagement along the way.

Organization

If in doubt, reorganize. For some leaders the first step when confronted with a difficult issue is to re-arrange the groups and reporting relationships. This can be really frustrating especially when it's seen as the proverbial rearranging the deckchairs on the Titanic because the root issue (elephant) has been ignored. It is probably true that too much of organization design is done on the back of napkins or as a knee-jerk reaction to a situation or a person issue or result from capricious 10% staff cuts.

Organizational changes include shifts in roles and responsibilities, reporting relationships, and work hand-offs from one group to another. Just like everything else these are dynamic and need to be periodically updated to match other changes in markets, products, and/or our underlying systems. They don't need to be perfect but they do need to make sense.

It is easy for organization changes to result in cries of, "It's not fair." Sometimes the result is from lack of involvement in the process, lack of explanation of the intention or justification, and because sometimes it appears to just be a personality preference or poor decision. Leaders can also see this as unnecessary and inappropriate meddling with critical decisions that are not up for debate. When you feel dug in, you probably are.

So how does restructuring become inspirational? Let's start by making that part of our intention. This is a good lens to use to reduce the difficulty and make better decisions. If we remember that we have lots of inspirational methods then we may start to see some options.

The often used organization announcement that includes the background and justification for selection doesn't say at the end, "Call me to argue about it." It does provide the basis for the choice. It established the inspirational story.

When we can, we can also include impacted teams in organizational design. Especially in working on decision rights, roles and responsibilities and process hand-offs. We work on the process of organization definition. This shift actually takes care of unforeseen issues and irons out conflicts and is more engaging.

Planned flexibility

Sometimes things don't go as planned. If our plans are less ridged it happens less often. We use general frameworks to get down to specific results as we get closer to the goal. For example in project planning we can think of milestones as check boxes along the way to measure timelessness and hold teams accountable. We can also use them as fine-tuning points where we expect to make adjustments.

Ironically, if we practice to be too precise in any aspect of this work, we only increase the odds that we will miss the mark. This starts when we fall into prediction paralysis trying to model every contingency and collect every scape of data. While we do this the world turns and more data is created. We do need good assumptions to start with and clear intentions. As we get closer to the specific aspects of the desired change, we create space for those to be shaped by an expanding team of those who are closer to the work and have the know-how.

Don't confuse this with shooting from the hip. Remember that a sense of control is critical in all stages of change. We balance the level of specificity in our planning and direction to match the situation and people. We always are responsible for the total activity and we share with the others who will ultimately be accountable after implementation.

Our change planning also needs to include operation not just implementation. We can step back when the systems are running as needed by the people who are their normal operators. This is a reminder to always use the final intended managers and operators of any system or process as the change/implementation team whenever possible. Our goal should be the earliest transition to the new status quo and that is when it works.

Sense Making

Human behavior is guided by patterns. So how can we modify these patterns? We start with the reason to try. Our motivation. This is our realization of why we want to do this. Not just knowing that someone else expects it or demands it. It is coming to the conclusion that we might benefit or not and that in either case we will at least make an initial commitment to try. Our little start at willingness. Our inspirational efforts help grow this willingness.

We build new patterns through creating a story and picture of where we are headed and how we will get there. Connecting the dots between past and future, old and new, how I was successful before and how I will be in the future. One way to think about this is that we tell our change story and every time we tell it to a new group or person, we change the main character to them.

During a change we may need to have help in building the patterns through learning new skills and practicing until we are confident. This includes ensuring the support is there to provide feedback so we don't waste time practicing failure. Think of this as the training wheels we put on the system until the team can ride by themselves.

An important aspect of learning and practicing is to build a step-by-step approach that guides others. It is not enough to sell the end state. Focus on building success a step at a time, piece by piece. Don't leave anyone behind.

We also want to make this a social activity with persons who will need to work together in the new reality practicing together as they go. The shared experience will reinforce a shared story and cement social norms. By working together we also practice group interactions and test the dependencies further building trust in the change and the extended team.

Aligning the stars

As we make it change we also make sure it fits. Making things fit means ensuring we have aligned the effort in the broader organization universe of intention, operation, changes and priority. Alignment occurs at every phase of change management and throughout our change readiness efforts. We do our best to ensure that we are aware, linked, and mutually supportive with all of the other moving parts that make a complex system like a company.

Our strategic alignment starts with the most senior guiding intention within the organization. This is more than mission and vison statements or value lists. It is a true alignment with the agenda from the Board, CEO and most senior team. It still is just the two parts of any intention; what we want to do and who we want to be. I suspect that if you are like me you have worked in places where they had all the formal statements and strategic plans while the agenda was still a mystery.

One way to maintain alignment with an unspoken agenda is to ensure your intentions get a full vetting. While it might seem a bit inefficient it is often easier for people to be critical instead of creative. This is especially true if they haven't fully articulated a positon. Our review and refinement is a good start.

Organizations suffer from a constant malady I call the Conflict of Good Intentions. Everyone wants to do a good job, many want to slay dragons, most of us see something that needs changed. So often what looks like disagreeable conflict is really just good ideas jockeying for position. It is helpful to recognize the good intention and shift focus from value (everything is potentially valuable) to priority (some of it needs done now). This maintains good will, doesn't put a stopper in the pipeline of good ideas, and supports inspirational change readiness by encouraging contribution.

We do need to check for a conflict with other efforts at the formal strategy and goal level. We all know that those only represent a portion, and sometimes relatively small amount of work being done and planned. A good approach is to check with functions and business units who share the same issue and have some responsibility for the current operation of supporting elements. They may see it too and be thinking of solutions or even engaged in an initiative that is related. In any case, they will be important for our projects for support and possibly as scaling partners to extend the value of our efforts.

During change it is necessary to maintain alignment with motivators outside our inspirational efforts. This means aligning things like bonus structures, talent reviews, and other incentives. It also means following all of the applicable rules.

In a sense, the most important alignment effort a leader needs to accomplish is the one they have the most control over; their own behavior. In the discussion of change readiness we looked at trustworthiness and what we need to do to maintain that advantage. It starts for us by being in front of things. Having enough knowledge and practice with change so that we can accelerate our own process of sense making

While we need to get in front of what has/will happen. We can't get too far ahead. We must maintain our patience with telling the story as many times as needed. Explaining what is going on or planned as needed by others. Our job is to give others a tangible example of effort and change behavior, we are the role models. This may seem like a bit of a trick. By acknowledging and accepting that it is our job to be a role model, we take the required steps on the path of our own sense of control. Trick or not, it works for us and will work for others.

The approach we use to manage change depends on the situation, people, risk and potential value involved. Leading change efforts is a balancing act based on the realities of the situation you find yourself in and the many paths that may work. The inspirational path is a choice. It both simplifies the process through known activities and steps, and it makes us aware of how complex it can be.

An awareness of complexity isn't an excuse for inaction or reason to be afraid. Lots of things are complex. Many paths are unknown. Our job is to move forward and find the better future. This is the most difficult part of leadership and its greatest reward. If we consider that we spend a lifetime being who we want to be and that around half of that lifetime is spent at work, we are only being efficient in finding our life's meaning by being personally consistent. Our expression of our selves is what we do, wherever and however we do it.

The great source of personal conflict for most of us is not doing this, not having the alignment between our personal aspirations and what we do with our time. Does this mean that we are always doing what we want and that is always going to be easy and fun? Of course not, we know life is ups and downs for everyone. The person we want to be is an aspirational self who experiences up and downs (the things we do) in the way that helps us get closer to that personal aspiration of self (who we want to be).

This is true for us and for everyone else. Let that sink in for a moment. We are all responsible for finding our own bliss and some of us create situations that frame this experience for others because we manage their time and goals. While we can't make others happy we can be mutually supportive in the realization of the meaningful expression of ourselves through our work.

Chapter Seven
Sustain

Nothing is meant to last forever; however, we don't want it to fall apart right away. So what can we do to make change stick? Another trick question? Of course the answer is, "It depends." Some of the changes we do we can't wait to finish, take a lesson learned or two and move on. For example, an unpleasant personnel action or unpopular course correction. A rule of thumb is if it's accomplished its purpose and has no necessary continuing elements, then let's be done. The great majority of changes actually fall into this category of sufficiently complete and next please.

The truth is sometimes though we just don't know when to let go. Remember the discussion about marginalizing people for mistakes? A really good memory might be a blessing and a curse especially if we hold onto mistakes and slights. So we are back to the importance of knowing what done look likes and unless it has changed, being satisfied with finding it. Another great truth is encapsulated in the 80/20 rule. The observation that 80% of the value comes from 20% of customers. That's not to say get close and stop. No, go till done but don't get so enamored with a change project or process that you become stuck in phase one.

Take off the training wheels

There are changes that need dedicated efforts to cement them into the organization structure and process status quo. The first step to sustainability is to ensure that we are fully up to operating the new systems, using the new protocol, or functioning in the new structure. It's time to take down the scaffolding to see if it an stand on its own. This means that we have a period where we pay attention and let it run on its own. Outside of observing performance and feedback we let it run with the regular management structure and the designed approach and roles.

Depending on the risk we intervene if things start to wobble although not too quickly. We want the team to have a last period of success and confidence building. It is OK when the training wheels come off that they still are a little wobbly, the team will have a last boost from having done it on their own.

One element we do want to sustain is the narrative of what happened, why and who stepped up for the challenge. Organizational history is the collection of the stories we tell ourselves. The attributions for heroic deeds, the massive failures and the sense of belonging and connection found along the way.

This narrative is important. It becomes the self-talk we collectively have that helps or hinders future change efforts by establishing a self-fulfilling prophecy. Not everything goes well, and we aren't engaged in revisionist history to accomplish nefarious ends. We need to find the happy ending, or the moral in the story, or the worthy sacrifice. It is always there, it is up to us to find it and make it true. If we do, the organization and our team members will retell it until it sticks. We know that a compelling story is magic.

Burning the platform

Contrary to some change management approaches, we usually don't get to start with a burning platform. Things aren't so dire that we are motivated by the complete lack of choice and impending doom. Actually we are pretty lucky that's true as it speaks volumes to how poorly something has been led if it is the typical case.

While we may not start with a burning platform, we might want to end with a nice bonfire. As in the legends of yore, we land on the shore and burn the ships so that we can't go back. I know a bit dramatic imagery for an IT system implementation. We do need to remove the obsolete system, delete the old protocol, and give the new organization the time to work. When it needs to stick, look for the matches.

Don't blow it

We can be our own worst enemies. Snatching failure out of the jaws of success. It is useful as we think about this to remind ourselves that leaders create resistance, we can get ahead of ourselves and if it doesn't work, no matter what, we will have our own selves to blame. All things roll up in leadership.

We lay the groundwork for failure when we don't take it seriously, fail to create readiness, aren't sincere in our inspirational attempts, or don't adequately plan. Sometimes we get in too great a hurry and the timeline becomes more important than the outcome. Sometimes we spend too much time telling and too little asking others. We must avoid the need to be personally right at the cost of a better way that everyone else can see. We put on the Emperor's new clothes and show ourselves in a not too flattering organizational fashion show.

It is hard to be perfect at anything especially telling and creating the future. So be OK with making a mistake or two. Try not to take it personally and remember to extend the same courtesy to others. Stick with your intentions. If you drift off, come back. Keep walking the talk. Don't try to do it alone. Leading change is like a playing on a teeter-totter. It has its ups and downs and it's no fun to play by yourself.

Party time

It's all over but the party! Yes, it is time to celebrate although remember to not wait until the end. On long patrols at sea submarine crews have a special celebration at the half-way mark; Half-Way Night. There is a great meal and some good natured fun. They don't have celebrations when they get home - that is the celebration. The second half is often the hardest part so the celebration is preparation for more effort. We have the opportunity to celebrate at many points along the way such as at the completion of milestones. Remember to make this a continuous process, another tool in the inspirational approach.

We do want to reward our teams. Not just the dragon slayers. We also want to recognize the foot soldiers and folks behind our supply lines. Be generous with credit to the point where it almost reduces your credibility. The credibility challenge only comes when the wrong people are recognized, we don't mean it, or we get stingy with rewards.

Change situations are natural recognition incubators. They can provide visibility for individual and team effort. Successful change can lead to increased self-esteem, new career opportunities and maybe even a bonus. Remember to bake the cake to enjoy along with the Change Soup.

Chapter Eight
Believe

Once when I was teaching a change workshop for production teams at a company going through significant change, one somewhat snarling third-shift team member said in an aggressive fashion, "Yeah we're all just going to die aren't we?" What a great insight. My reply to him was, "That's right, so what are you going to do between now and then?"

There is a great change story from the Tao Te Ching about a farmer and his son. The farmer and his son are very poor and barely getting by. One morning they discover that their horse has run away, leaving them to work their fields by hand. The neighbors come over and say, "What a terrible thing has happened." The farmer responds, "Maybe."

Soon the horse comes back with two more horses. The neighbors rush over to congratulate the farmer on his good fortune. "You are rich, what a great thing." The farmer responds, "Maybe."

The son starts to attempt to break one of the horses and is thrown off and he breaks his leg. The neighbors rush over and say "how terrible that this has happened to you, now things are worse than before," The farmer's response, "Maybe."

Just a week or two later, the Army comes through the village and take all of the young men to war, but they don't take the farmer's son because of the broken leg. Again the neighbors come over and say, "how lucky you are that your son is spared this danger" and again the farmer responds, "Maybe."

I'm sure you have figured out that this could go on and on. The point is that often we can't really see the outcome of an event for a long time, and as time passes it is difficult to tell exactly what contributed to the end result anyway. Have you ever had the experience of looking back on your life and thinking, now I see why that happened? It all seems to make sense now when at the time it made no sense at all.

Creating change is the core work of leaders but no one can predict the future. We will die, but that isn't an excuse to give up or do nothing because of all of the "maybes" that could or might happen. As leaders we have to make decisions and move forward.

The good news is that we can improve our odds of change success and we have that opportunity every day. It is a choice in the face of uncertainty to choose an inspirational path. It is also a choice to maintain our commitment to being who we aspire to be even when it is hard to see the immediate value. Let us be encouraged. If we maintain our intentions we will bring the magic in our change soup.

Professional believers

Let's remember the story of Stone Soup and the real magic the soldiers brought. Of course it wasn't a stone. It wasn't the compelling story either. It was that they believed and shared their belief with others. They believed that there would be something to eat. They believed that they could engage others to do something they didn't believe themselves. The gift they left was a measure of belief for tomorrow.

We will never realize our intentions if we don't start by believing they are possible. Management can seem like a cold and mechanistic process devoid of magic and even humanity. We learn systems and processes and formulas to guide us. There is something more fundamental, more important; it is the spark of belief.

We must believe in three things to turn this spark into fire. First we must believe in ourselves. Give yourself permission and have the confidence that you can make a difference and achieve your intentions. Secondly, believe in your organization, understand the direction and needs and know that you and your team can help. Finally, you must believe in the people who depend on you; your reporting staffs and teams. There are few things more inspirational than someone who believes in us.

Creating a Legacy

Every day we are practicing being who we want to be. Sometimes that practice is mindful, sometimes not so much. It is important to realize that our "every days" are actually what prepares us for the big days, and maybe our greatest achievements are in-between all of the obvious big projects. This is how we create change readiness.

I once had a new job as a college professor and I was working to make some changes to the program classes in my area. A visibly upset colleague, who had originally built the curriculum and was now close to retirement called me to her office. "What are you doing?" "Your changes will ruin my legacy."

As she spoke I realized that the legacy she would have when she left wasn't the design of the program or even if they named a building in her honor. Her legacy was the achievements and love from all the students she had touched during her career.

The important lesson I took from that day, and for which I am forever grateful, is that in each day, and in fact every interaction, we can create what we desire. That in the end our story isn't based on our grand plans and major achievements but is in fact the total of all of those seemingly unimportant interactions and decisions we make every day.

Every day we practice being who we want to be and making the difference we want to see

Made in the USA
Monee, IL
23 June 2020